Flowing Passion

To Aunt Easter
Thank you for your
love and support.
You are the best! I
Pray this book inspires you.
Keep your passion Flowing
May God richly bless you
always
Love always
Anita

Flowing Passion

Bold, Beautiful and Inspiring Words

Anita A. Hymes

Library of Congress Control Number:		2011914474
ISBN:	Hardcover	978-1-4653-4874-6
	Softcover	978-1-4653-4873-9
	Ebook	978-1-4653-4875-3

This book was printed in the United States of America.

To order additional copies of this book, contact:
Xlibris Corporation
1-888-795-4274
www.Xlibris.com
Orders@Xlibris.com
102849

CONTENTS

DEDICATIONS

This book is dedicated to my father, Bishop James Hymes, My late mother, Angelena Green Hymes and my son Kirkland "DJ" Grant for their continuous prayers, support, Unconditional love and encouragement. This book is a reality because of them and God!

Author, Anita A. Hymes

WORDS FROM THE AUTHOR . . .

"Flowing Passion" is a book of bold, beautiful and inspiring poems and creative writings created over the course of four years. My writings are based on life experiences; it is my creative truth, seen through my eyes. I am sure that you will be able to relate to one or more of the poems. I pray that this book inspires and uplifts you!

Every poem that I write changes my perception and forces me to face reality. It helps me to learn, and grow in all areas of my life. Every poem I write stirs a passion in me and broadens my creativity and imagination. It creates a new me. I write to create my mind and to heal my soul . . . Writing is truly healing to my soul!

One of my favorite quotes I live by is: "I have learned that success is to be measured not so much by the position that one has reached in life as by the obstacles which he has over come while trying to succeed". ~Booker T. Washington. Writing this book, "Flowing Passion" helped me to overcome many obstacles in my life by healing myself with Bold, Beautiful and Inspiring words.

Faith is the dream of becoming something you can't touch but only dream of. Without faith nothing is possible, with it nothing is impossible. ~Anita Hymes. This book is possible only because of my faith and prayers. Keep your faith flowing!

ACKNOWLEDGMENTS . . .

Above all, praises, honor, and glory goes to the King of Kings and Lord of Lords. I praise God for giving me the vision, skills and bold, beautiful and inspiring words for writing this book. I thank Him for waking me up in the middle of the night with flowing words and titles to use in this book.

My heartfelt appreciation goes out to all of my family, and friends who inspired me to write this book and who prayed for me and believed in me when I couldn't see this day.

Special thanks to my father Bishop James Hymes, who encouraged me always, taught me about courage and strength, inspired me and prayed for me day and night. Love you daddy! I give my honor and respect to my late mother, Mrs. Angelena Green Hymes who planted the good seeds, gave Godly advice and guidance at a very young age and set good examples for me to follow. To my son Kirkland "DJ" Grant, thank you for believing that I can do anything and for pushing me to reach my goals. Thanks for critiquing my work and giving good advice on the book title and for loving me and caring about me unconditionally. I am so proud of you for never giving up on anything and for standing by my side always. I love you very much son!

To my dear one and only sister whom I love deeply, Dr. Amy Hymes thank you for encouraging me, inspiring me, motivating me and praying for me and with me. Thanks for giving me free professional advice when I needed it most. To my brothers Gerald and Troy Hymes, thanks for believing in me, loving me and keeping me grounded and real. Much love for both of you! To my nieces and nephews thanks for looking up to me, trusting me and believing in me: Tamar "Quaz", Brandon, Takeyah, Troy Jr., Diamond, Angelena, Shanya, and Sydnee I love you all so much! My gratitude goes to my special Aunties and uncle who has always been there for me and encouraged me; Ms Easter LaRoche, Lydia Simmons, Rev Lillian Washington and Frankie Hymes. I love you all!

Very special thanks to my Special Friends: *To Glenn Robinson for your support, many lessons, and for inspiring me to make this book a reality. Thanks for teaching me how to fly! To Uche Lebeanya for being such a great friend! For never giving up on me and for staying in touch with me over the years. Thanks for inspiring me to see more and do more! To Maurice Burton for believing in me, uplifting me, and inspiring me to write poems and seeing through "new eyes". You all have touched my heart in such a profound and unique way. Because of you I am better! You have been a big part of my inspiration in writing this book. Thanks for your many lessons and support. I Love you all forever!*

Extra special thanks to my "True" friends *who stuck with me through good times and bad times and never left my side. For helping me see my true worth and for showing me unconditional love everyday and believing in me. For praying for me and with me . . . My "True" Friends Jackie Bradsher, Yvonne Sanders, Mary Pleasant, Essence LaBoy, Octavia McBride, Barbara Chisholm, , Lyn Bird, Alice Cunningham, Reginald Williams, Brother Man and Eddie Kidd. You all will never know how much you mean to me and how much you have touched my life in such a positive way and for that I am eternally grateful! I love you all!*

My ongoing devotion goes to my pastor Jason L Johnson of Abundant Life Evangelistic Center, Biloxi Ms for preaching God's word every Sunday. Through God's words you have encouraged me and motivated me to have "faith" and not give up. You have inspired me to go "higher". Because of your teaching this book is a reality!

My applause and sincere appreciation goes to Kirkland "DJ" Grant for photos used in this book. To Ira LaRoche and Maxwell Cooley, for their artistic creations and contribution to this book, and for creating through my eyes. Special thanks to Mr. Cooley for stepping in at the last minute and creating such great art. You are the best! To Easter LaRoche for her many hours of editing this book and Glenda Lewis and my publishing team @ Xibris for keeping me on track and making this book a reality.

Contributing Artists:
Maxwell Cooley, Artist
Ira LaRoche, Artist
Kirkland "DJ" Grant, Photography

Contribution:
Acknowledgement of my beautiful niece, Miss Angelena Hymes, for the photo of her sitting in the Angel Oak Tree. Gullah Girl page 46.

Again, thanks to all of my family and friends for being such a special part of my life and for supporting me, encouraging me and inspiring me to make this book a reality today. May God richly bless you all . . . I love you all for eternity! Keep it Flowing!

"FLOWING PASSION"

I boldly stir my passion deep with in me, releasing my creativity into a mighty explosion allowing greatness to flow out of me. My passion leaps with excitement every time my story is told. It flows like flowing water with bold, beautiful and inspiring words; it is my truth, seen through my eyes for eternity.

You Inspired ME

*You have inspired me to be the Godly women I
am . . . You prayed for me and with me, you helped
me and walked with me. You encouraged me, you
loved me and you supported me, you told me that I am
special, you told me that I am beautiful, you told me
that I am smart, you told me that I was creative from
the very start.*

*You inspired me to dream big . . . You believed in me
and you saw great things in me. You pushed me to reach
higher limits and reminded me to never give in, and
never let my dreams die inside. You told me to go for
it and reach the top with leaps and bounds, you said I
deserved only the best and I said Oh, yes! You said a life
fit only for a queen is what I should dream.*

You inspired me to do great things . . . You told me I have what it takes to climb high mountains and do the impossible things. You told me I can do it despite the attack of my enemies. You helped me rise above adversities and ignored the negativity. You cried with me when I fell and helped me up, but didn't let me stay down for a long time. I heard your gentle voice say, "come on my pretty child, stand tall, here it comes, lets try it again . . . I know you can do it!" You pushed me up the success ladder holding me up with your prayers, lessons, and encouragement. As I flew around the world visiting places I have only dreamed of seeing, you looked down with a smile of approval saying yes, that's my child!

You inspired me to love more . . . Your unconditional love, your touch, your kindness, your guidance, your attentiveness, your loyalty, your dedication, your passion and your gentleness all showed me true love. You gave your heart to show me true love and to let me feel what love should be, so I didn't have to search the world to see.

You inspired me to pray more . . . You taught me to take the time to thank God daily for the great life he has bestowed upon me. I praise him for all his blessings and greatness I have lived to see. I thank Him for the small things, the big things and for the mighty miracles I see in my life today. And when adversities come and I don't know what to do or say, I remember your words, "fear not and don't fall apart, but trust in His words and continue to pray!" You taught me to fall on my knees and call on Jesus' name for guidance every day. You said no matter what happens trust God, NEVER GIVE UP and never give in!

Angel Mommy, you inspired me to become a Godly Woman, Dream Big, Do Great Things, Love More, Pray More and Never Give Up! You are my inspiration today and always!

Dedicated to my Mother and Angel, Mrs. Angelena Green Hymes

Healing a Broken Heart

I wonder why we have to suffer for love. Is it to teach us something and make us strong? Why does love hurt so badly at times? Is it to remind us of our wrong?

I am an emotional wreck, deeply wounded by what I thought was love. I am miserable and don't understand what went so wrong between the two.

My heart bleeds with hurt, disappointment, sadness and denial. It's ripped apart and cracked into million pieces.

It's damaged from distrust, lies, pride and competition. All the things I never knew existed. It brings discontent and discomfort to my life. I must find a way to heal my fragile heart and get it right. I can not stay in the valley for too long for I don't want to start singing the pity song.

Now, how do I begin to heal a broken heart and move on? First, it's about forgiveness even if you don't love me any more. No time for blaming, judging or bashing him because it only hurts more deeply and delays the healing. I will never utter a negative thing because with God's help ultimately I'm going to win.

I pray for forgiveness for all the wrong between the two. I release it all and now I am ready to do what I need to do. No need for guilt, shame or blame, it's time to keep it flowing and start all over again. I have tossed resentment, and judgment, it's about forgiveness again. Today is a new beginning with many new opportunities; I will rise up in love and try it again because healing is here to stay!

Illustrated by Maxwell Cooley

A Lady

She is graceful, elegant and sophisticated too. She turns heads when she walks into a room from her aura and beauty, she is a lady.

She is a step above them all because God dwells within. She is so kind and understanding when she deals with things, she is a lady.

She takes care of her business and she is right on time. She is always honest and true to those who she loves, she is a lady.

She never breaks under pressure for she knows where her help comes from, she is a lady.

She is everything to everyone she knows. She gives and gives of herself and expects nothing in return. She prays for her man, her children and her family continuously, she is a lady.

She is one of a kind and yes; she will blow your mine. She is a lady.

A Good Man

I looked around me to find a good man. He is one who is **strong** and **caring** and He is true and **honest** to the core. He stands up for what is right and he fights and fights with all his might. He never gives up to defeat and he never misses a beat. He shows **confidence** in all He does and He never tries to compete with his lady. He is in it to win it until the end because he is **loyal** to his family and friends.

He shows **unconditional love** and **kindness** in a very **unique** way. He is always here to stay because he is **committed** in every way. He **loves his mother** and family with all his might and shows **respect** with all he does. He is **free from drama** and keeps it real. He is not always rich and full of fame but he represents **greatness** just the same. See money does not define who he really is, it's what's in his heart that tells his story and all can see his glory.

His **inner beauty** shines so bright. He is more **beautiful** than a king. He is **dedicated** to his calling and inspires all those he comes in contact with. He is very **dependable** and never lets his family down. He shows **strength, patience**, and **calmness** when he faces adversity because he knows how to face reality.

He **loves the Lord** and **prays** and prays and worships Him in his own unique way. He asks God for a better day as he travels on his way. Oh yes, we have good men all around us everyday . . . Our husbands, our man, our friends, our sons, our fathers, our brothers, our cousins, our uncles, and our nephews are all good men, so let's lift them up high, praise them and treat them as a king in everyway!

Illustrated by Ira LaRoche

I am Wonder Woman

I felt the enormous hurt, the awful shame, the deep pain, the extreme disappointment and the shocking embarrassment you brought to me. It pierces my heart so deeply and I continued to weep into the mid nights.

I know I must not allow my thoughts to define myself by your definition of me. I am much more than what you have made me to be. I am like wonder woman you see. I leap over hurt, I pray over the shame, I soar above disappointment, and I fly high over embarrassment.

I am much more than what you see in me, I am like Wonder Woman, I am mighty as can be. I am much more than how you treated me, I am strong you see. I am like Wonder Woman all the power lives in me.

I flow with strength and power so I know, "this too shall pass". I am like Wonder Woman you see, so you can't touch me!

My True Friend

You are my rock and truth. You help me to be strong and keep it real. You are my support, cheerleader, and advocate. You believed in me and promoted me and you never left me. You are my sounding board when I need to go off. You are everything to me . . . You are my true friend.

You are my ear when I can not hear the truth. You are my eyes when I can not see the way to go, you are my voice when I am too weak to speak. You are my strength when I want to give up and give in. You are everything to me . . . You are my true friend.

You show me unconditional love and look for nothing in return. You stood by my side and never left me even when I was wrong. You pick me up when I am down and take me to higher grounds. You push me to go all the way and never let me stay. You celebrate my successes and accomplishments with excitement in every way. You cry with me when I am hurt and sad and laugh with me when I am happy. You laugh at me when I am silly and make me feel so good about myself. You pray with me and for me when I need it most and you never let me lose hope. You are everything to me, you are my true friend.

You always see the best in me when I can't see my worth. You pick me up and stand tall with me when I fall. You celebrate me for just being me when I could not see my true beauty. You still love me even though you know the true me. My secrets are always safe with you and your lips are tightly sealed. You over look my moodiness and never judge me for my many mistakes. You understand my weaknesses and help me to be stronger in this race. You are everything to me . . . You are my true friend.

You give 100% unconditional love in every way! Praise God for sending my BFF my way. You are my everything, you are my true friend!

The Wings of a Beautiful Butterfly

My wings are open wide and it feels so free to me. I have experienced the highs and lows of the beautiful butterfly and felt the deep depth of love, even if it was just for a little while and didn't match my life style.

You see, I now know what true love can really be . . . It looks like the beauty of the colorful wings of a butterfly . . . It feels like the excitement of the height of a beautiful butterfly as it spread it's wings wide and fly high . . . It smells like the sweet aroma of a lily flower as the butterfly flies in the garden . . . It tastes like the very sweet nectar of a flower.

I must not fear, harbor hate, worry, stress, or lose faith just because my beautiful butterfly flew away. I must let my beautiful butterfly be free so it can spread its beautiful wings and share its true beauty, and love again with no shame, no regrets, no fears, no hesitations, and no doubts.

If by chance my beautiful butterfly happens to return to me one day, I will embrace it with love; then I know with NO doubt it was truly meant for "ME" and only me!
Be free, spread your wings, and fly high my beautiful butterfly . . . Fly High with Love . . .

Illustrated by Maxwell Cooley

My Angel Watched over me . . .

*She watched over me and protected me; she held me in
her arms and didn't let me die. She pleaded my case to
the master up high. And yes, of course I survived. She
said you will live because you have work to do with a
mighty story to tell them too.*

*Go forth in love with excitement and encourage them
all! Use your skills and motivate them too.*

*She said you were given the voice, imagination, and pen
to use; so I have no choice but to spread the good news!*

I Surrender

The love of my life you are, the void in my heart you filled. You brought me joy, laughter, happiness, and brighter days. Oh, yes you did!

Today I wait, look and wonder with heavy heart to see what's coming my way. I will remain silent! I can not beg . . . I will not plead because God must be in total control. I give up my power, I give up my voice. I fall on my knees and tell God to please take full control.

It must be done in love. It must be done with respect. It must be done in peace because we are lovers who begun our journey together with "mighty prayers" then our Angels made plans for us to meet.

You touched my heart in great ways. You taught me great things. Our love journey must not be forgotten. Our "Angelic" meeting must not be in vain, even though it did not sustain.

It was a true love with flames that burned bright that we allowed to fade away. We some how lost our fire, could it be that we allowed self to get in the way? So what should we do? Perhaps, one day we can rekindle that hot fire that brought us together!

In the meantime, remember my Smile, remember my Laugh. Remember my gentle Touch, remember my Kisses and remember my Love . . . But most of all remember the positive words I uttered to you . . . I Love You!

International Man

*Wow! His voice was so sexy and pleasing to my ear.
His smile was as bright and enchanting as the light.
His face was handsome and painted with boldness. I
listened to him with intensity and drifted away with
his mystery.*

*He was so polite and kind it blew my mind because I
had never met anyone of his kind. He taught me many
new things and yes it was out of sight. He showed me
new ways to do things and his new ideas made me very
bright. He broadens my horizon in so many ways. We
bonded like glue and he became my true friend and
confidant too. We shared secrets that we will never tell
a sole; we shared many ideas and learn so much more.
We had so much fun and laughter's that erupted with
glorious times.*

*He was smart and well traveled, which inspired me
to see and do more. He was confident in all he did; he
convinced me to see through his eyes. He handled me
with such great zest, it gave me joy and excitement and
I cannot settle for less. He read and traveled the world
afar and did not rest. He cooked his native food for me
just to give me a taste of what he loved most and to stir
my imagination of his homeland so far. The thrill and
mysteries of my international man's life intrigues me
more and more everyday.*

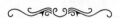

Dear Woman of God

*Continue to be strong and walk in faith for God will
never leave or forsake you. He loves you more than life
because you are so precious in His sight.*

*Now, praise God for His favor upon your life and praise
Him all day long. Praise Him for all the mighty blessings
he brought to your life as you hum your song. Praise
Him with a pen and paper and write it all day long.*

*You are a mighty woman in God's sight and oh how He
delights. Expect nothing less than impressiveness; expect
Him to do great and powerful things in your life. For I
know He cares about you more than life. He is able to
do the impossible things and perform miracles like no
one else can do.*

*Don't let the haters and negative ones bring you down
for God will always be around. Don't allow them to
make you second guess yourself or doubt your worth.
They are so jealous of your greatness and great work!*

*Don't be judged by their standards for they all want to
see you fall, but remember God wants you to have it
all! Don't allow anyone to dictate your future and tell
you what you can not do because you have the strength
to bring it through.*

*Never forget your worth and how valuable you truly
are. So many people love you and look up to you by far.
You are worthy for all greatness and praises . . . You are
a mighty woman of God!*

Silence

Your Silence has made me curious. It has caused me to think, wonder, assume, and second guess myself.

Your silence sounds so loud in my ear without speaking a word. It is so quiet but still speaks boldly to me. Your silence sends a clear and confusing message . . . It says rejection, disconnection, and disinterest.

As the seconds, minutes, hours, days, weeks, and months passes by with silence, I wonder how could this be and do you ever think of me?

I have lost hope in something I once called mine. I am convinced with every passing day that your silence speaks volume and the real truth that lies inside. I now embrace that truth about silence and stop denying reality. Your silence cuts so deep and it will never make me complete.

Celebrating My Freedom

I am taking my life back; I am taking my confidence back too! And I am taking my power back because I am free to be me. No restrictions just being me. I will do as I want and come as I please. I only need to answer to myself, God, and only me. I don't need any man to validate me, especially if he wants to keep a hold on me. I make my own decisions and free to do things my way, of course only after I pray, so he will never control me.

I jump for joy and my heart is filled with laughter. I can go where I want, get what I want and be who I am only because no one has a hold on me. I am free to be me!

Loving a Man With Mighty Pain and Rage

At first he was so nice, he was so kind, so attentive to me it blew my mind! He had so much patience with me, so I just knew he was going to be mine for eternity so I didn't realize. Then he became irate, he became agitated, he even cried, but I still didn't realize.

He blamed me, He yelled at me, he stomped his feet, he walked out on me and he told me it was all my fault, then later he apologized with a hug and kiss and yes, I was remiss because I still didn't realized.

The anger, the rage, the mood swings, the highs and lows how could I not realize? He exploded, then he became depressed; He cried and sobbed upon my breast. For a while I thought I would lose my mind. Finally, after I prayed, watched, and waited. I said "Oh my God" now I realize!!

The pain and battles with his struggle was suddenly so apparent to me. I fell on my knees and I prayed and ask God to please help me. I prayed day and night for Him . . . Dear Lord, please heal my friend and set Him Free!

Persistence is Me

*I know I must always be persistent in all I do and I
know that God will see me through. God sees it all and
knows all of my fears. He will bring me through if I
trust in him and be persistent all my days.*

*My mother told me to stand up, be strong, fight for
what I wanted and never give into defeat! She said,
"Have friend, trust few learn to paddle my own canoe".*

*You have taken away the things that belong to me, and
the thing I wanted so badly. You hurt me and made me
cry. Then I realized it was only momentarily if it was
truly given from God. If I remain persistent until the
truth is told, God will vindicate me, oh how I know.*

*Oh, NO! I can't give up, I can't give in. I must work
harder, pray harder and be persistent in all I do.
I know if I give up now and give into the world's
definition of me. I will let those people down who
prayed for me.*

*I can't let big momma, big papa, mommy, daddy, my
son, my sister, my brothers, my man, and my dedicated
family and friends down. I must show strength and be
persistent even if I am knocked down yet again.*

*Yes, I heard the words "NO", "Denied", "Rejected",
"Stop", "Delayed" and then for a moment I thought
to myself, maybe I was not good enough, smart enough,
light enough, small enough, pretty enough and I wanted
to cry. But then I remembered, on this journey I must
be persistent and never let my dreams die.*

You said I couldn't do it, you said I couldn't have it, you said I couldn't get it, you said I couldn't reach it, you said I couldn't make it, you said I couldn't survive it. I asked you why??? You told me because I was not good enough, I wasn't smart enough, I wasn't the right color, and I wasn't a good fit.

I replied, "Excuse me", but you must not know whose child I am . . . I will prove you wrong just wait as I weather the storm.

Yes, you tried to hold me back and hold me down, by lying on my name, undermining me, and backstabbing me just to steal what was mine. I guess you didn't realize that I was persistent in all I do and I am a true child of the highest God, but I'm sure you will see in time.

That's when I heard my father whisper, "Child well done, take a rest, and I'll step in and clear up this mess". As I look at my life today, I say persistence paid off in a big way!

I have It, All You See . . .

Patient with fervent prayer
Energy to run the race to get there
Reality to see my dreams come true.
Success for me it's true
Invent the real strength and truth in me
Strive to be better everyday!
Tenacity to hope and dream for more
Encourage myself to get up and go
Never give up, even when I am done wrong
Call on the Lord's name night and day
Endure to the end and I will see . . . My
persistency brought me victory

Now you see . . . Persistence is me!

No More!

No more drama, no more pain, no more disappointments, no more lies, no more playing games . . . I throw them all away! No more sadness, no more worries, no more fear, no more begging and pleading, no more fights, no more giving up . . . I leave them all behind! No more leaving me, no more embarrassments, no more negativity, no more settling for less, no more waiting . . . I delete them from my history! Today is a new day and I will take my life back and take a stand and say no more! No More! NO MORE!

Amazing Promises for a Woman of Hope

I wait, I hope, I see, I pray I embrace it with expectation of assurance, yes I do!

Promises of Peace, Promises of Joy, and Promises of Justice, Promises of calmness, quietness, truth and faith are things I hold too, even though sometimes it seems not true.

I cry, I weep, I scream, I mourn, and then I ask "why"? Then suddenly I realize my promises of a better tomorrow will come true! It's hard you know, but it's true! Promises of a better tomorrow will come true!

Those promises are so near to me and, oh it's so true. I stand up and say "NO to defeat!

Fear, Anger, Pity, Defeat and Shame can only minimize the truth of the promises I know to be true.

I regret nothing because my promises are so true. It holds truth in my heart. Yes! I know it will do.

Dry your eyes and lift up your head, rise up women of hope! Move forward with boldness, power and strength remembering these traits are deeply imbedded within from your ancestors.

WHY WHY WHY

Why do we give up and give in when things don't go our way? Why don't we stand up and fight for what God has given us?

Why do we hurt each other when we love them so much? Didn't our parents taught us better than that? So, tell me why do we do it over and over again? I wonder if we really know what we are doing. Is it intentional or is it unintentional? Never the less why do we do it? Are we not strong mighty people of great faith and strength? Didn't the preacher prayed for our union? So why are we not stronger than the ordinary people and why do we settle for defeat?

Tell me why? Can we not see the hurt, the pain, and the disappointment we bring those who look up to us and love us so much? Why can't we just get it together and love each other for eternity?

Why? So, what's really going on? Is it pride? Is it lack of faith? Is it defeat? Is it selfishness? Is it fear? Is it arrogant? Is it a Power struggle? Or is it an attack of the enemy to separate the family that God has put together? Must we transform ourselves to be like the negative hurting world, or can we rise up and make a stand to be better and different for all?

Why can't we see the hurt and sadness in God's eyes as we give up and give in? Have we not called on his holy name for help or must we continue to hold on to pride doing it our way?

Dear husband, didn't we say The Lord brought us together? So why didn't we ask Him to keep us together? Why should we continue to bear the burden of doing things our way and hurting our children as we play? Is our way His way? Is our way the right way? Have we tried forgiveness, unconditional love and togetherness? Why do we continue to do what we do when God's way is the only way? Why, Why, Why?

My Vision

*My VISION of tomorrow is so bright because I can see
God shinning His light upon my life. It shines so clear
so I know he's near, therefore I need not fear. My Vision
of tomorrow is filled with Greatness, Happiness, Hope,
Peace, Love, Joy, Faith, Anticipation, Excitement,
Emotions and Glory. The days ahead are ones I will
embrace with open arms as I travel on my journey.*

*I can dream big so I can envision all of the great things
in stored for me. I see bright blue skies, the shinning
sun, beautiful designs, blue beaches, white sands,
beautiful flowers, the hot weather, romantic music with
slow dance, his big strong arms wrapped around me to
comfort me and protect me, his great big smile looking
at me with tender kisses just for me, and him falling in
love with only me. Yes! I can see.*

*My dreams and Visions of a better tomorrow are
finally coming true. I am elated and praise God for
coming through. He has given me my heart desires and
now my heart will forever be on fire, burning so strong
because of a Vision I dreamed of so long.*

My life seems so complete only because of his unique ways he speaks. He tells me I am beautiful, he tells me that I am special, he tells me that I am good, he tells me that I am smart, he tells me that I am respectful, he tells me that he loves me, and then I start to smile and say WOW, thank you God for letting me see my Vision of a better tomorrow even if it's just for a little while . . .

At last, that VISION I only dreamed of, prayed for, and hoped for is my reality today!

He was Here for a "REASON"

Please don't cry and get mad with Him! He has done his time, don't you realize? He was here for a "Reason" and his purpose is done. You have learned all you can from him so it's time for him to move on and run.

He's not a bad man, it's not his fault! He loved you, He taught you so many things, He helped you, He supported you when you needed it most, and He brought you joy and fun; but today his reason is done!

Wonderful Are YOU!

Warms my soul
Offer assistance
Nice to me
Dedicated to me
Eager to please me
Right on time
Faithful and fun
Unbelievable
Loving

You are so **WONDERFUL TOO ME!**

Photo Taken by Kirkland "DJ" Grant Jr.

Gullah Girl

Girl, don't let those people pull you down and allow them to tell you what to do and where to stay. Big mamma gave you a voice so stand up for yourself. You know you are strong if you could have worked in the fields all day long. Remember your past when you had to pick tomatoes in the fields and shelled those beans just to make means.

It's a new day now, you have a voice and power because you have knowledge and education to share with all. Just stand up and let those people see your might because you made it through the fight.

You are free to be who you once only dream of becoming. You are free to go to places you only saw in your imagination or read in a book. You are free to own your own business that you never saw how. You are free to own your own beautiful home that you once fantasized about. You are free to drive in a fine luxury car and forget about the hoopdee you once knew. You are free to write a book for all to read and see and to inspire them to become who they want to be. Who would ever imagine that would be, little old me from a dirt road and Angel Oak tree.

Just stand up and don't let them people put you down again because we know you made it from the ground to the stars only because of prays afar. It's a new day Gullah girl; you can do it in a big way!

Common Gullah Phrases

Uh mean fuh do so	*I meant to do it*
See um da.	*See it there.*
Bring em yuh.	*Bring it here.*
I ein know.	*I don't know*
I ein been know.	*I really don't know it .*
Wha fuh?	*What for?*
I got da misery ein my head.	*The pain is in my head*
Muh head da hut me	*My head is hurting me*
Trow em ober da.	*Throw it over there.*
Who pa you?	*Who is your father?*
Ova ya.	*Over there*
She do em fo she.	*She did it for her*
She do em fo e left.	*She did it before she left*
Oh, you eim been know dat?	*Oh' you didn't know that?*
E been don dead.	*He has been dead for some time*
Who dat in da?	*Who's that in there?*
Yiddie me.	*I heard it*
Yuh so.	*I heard it*
Wha Hunnah da do ein da?	*What are you all doing in there?*
Wha e been yat?	*Where was he/she*
How much e fa?	*How much is it?*
Wha time dag wine ein da crick	*What time are we going in the creek*
Da pot da bile	*The pot is boiling*
Him bex	*Is he angry*
Who dem flowiz fa?	*Who are the flowers for?*
Hush da nize.	*Be quiet*
How'l ole e is?	*How old is he?*
Hunnah da lie!	*You all are lying*

Him eye long.	*He is greedy*
You yent.	*You lie*
Him say him da man.	*He says he is a man*
Him smell him man	*He's flirting /being nasty*
Him say him fuh married	*He says he wants to get married*
How ole is she	*How old is she?*
No olda; no younger. Jus' so.	*The same age as he is now*
Ya mout tink	*Your mouth smells bad*

"Angel Oak Tree, John's Island SC"

"Sweet Grass Basket Weaving"

Gullah Gal—Gullah translation

Gal, doe let dem people pull ya down and let dem tell ya wha fa do an way fa stay. Big mamma gee ya ah voice so stand up fa ya self. Ya know ya strong if ya couda wok in da fields till sun rise and sun down. Memba ya pass when huna had fa pic dem matas in da fields and shell dem beans jus fa make um. E ah new day now, ya hafa voice and powa cas ya got education fa share wit all dem. Jus stand up and let dem people see ya power cus ya made em thew da fight. Ya free fa be who ya dream bout. Ya free fa go whay ya see in ya magination an read in ah book. Ya free fa own ya own pretty house that ya thout bout long time. Ya free fa own ya own bussiness ya neva tout wouda be. Ya free fa drive in ah fine luxury kar and fagot bout the hoopdee ya had. Ya free fa rite eh book fa all ta read an see. Who wouda eva thout dat wouda been, lil ol me from ah dut road an Angel Oak Tree. Jus stand up an doe let dem people put ya down gain cause da no ya made um from the ground to da sky jus cas ol people bena pray fa ya. E ah new day Gullah gal; ya can do um yo way.!!!

Why Do I Love You?

I love you because God sent you to me . . .
I love you because you are a Godly man . . .
I love you because you pray for me and with me . . .
I Love you because you inspire me . . .
I love you because you are strong . . .
I love you because you are confident . . .
I live you because you are honest . . .
I love you because you tell me I am beautiful . . .
I love you because you treat me like a queen . . .
I Love you because you love me so much . . .
I love you because you are in love with me . . .
I love you because you won the approval of my Father . . .
I love you because you make me feel so special . . .
I love you because you are so special . . .
I love you because you encourage me . . .
I love you because you support me . . .
I love you because you motivate me . . .
I love you because we have fun together . . .
I love you because you care about me . . .
I love you because you love me just as I am . . .
I love you because you have patience with me . . .
I love you because you love me even when I am in a nasty mood . . .
I love you because you are willing to help me with anything . . .
I love you because you try so hard . . .
I love you because you make me happy . . .

I love you because you make me laugh and smile . . .
I love you because you are so sexy . . .
I love you because I am so attracted to you . . .
I love you because we look really good together . . .
I love you because our family and friends knows that we belong together . . .
I love you because you have taught me so much . . .
I love you because you satisfy me . . .
I love you because you make me feel safe . . .
I love you because you taught me so much . . .
I love you because you have made me a better person . . .
I love you because no one has ever loved me this way . . .

I love you more than you will ever know!

You Failed Me

*I am so disappointed because you did not protect me
nor did you take care of me. I gave you my heart and
my daddy gave you my hands and you did not protect
me. How could that be? You failed me as a person, you
failed me as a woman, you failed me as a friend, you
failed me as a girlfriend, you failed me as your fiancé
and you failed me as your wife! How do I begin to
forgive you for your failures and move on with my life?
If Jesus can forgive our sins, surely I can forgive you for
your passion. For you are only a man!*

Celebrating an Angel Named Gerri

You are our Angel, so beautiful and sweet you are. You are our Angel and heaven needed you there.

Angel Gerri, we see your beaming smile with beautiful silky white wings open wide. Sprinkled with colors of gold, red, and blue just right for only you.

You are our Angel you brought us love. You are our Angel you brought us comfort and peace, you are our Angel you brought us friendship and laughs.

Now today My Angel Gerri we miss you so much words can't express our broken heart.

We know that heaven is celebrating your homecoming and we are too. Oh, but how we long for and wish we could get just one more touch, just one more kiss, just one more hug, just one more smile from that Angelic face that we all adored so much.

You are our Angel Gerri. We will never forget your love and lessons you stamped in our hearts. We promise, your dreams and spirit will live on and on inside us all.

Now, Angel Gerri spread your beautiful wings graced with that Angelic face and radiant smile.

Spread your wings wide and fly high. Fly fly, fly high you beautiful Angel fly high . . .

Until we meet again in heaven Angel Gerri Spread your beautiful wings like an eagle and soar . . . fly high as we look on with a smile and a tear in our eye and say Goodbye!

Special Prayer of Deliverance for My Friend

Father God, in the name of Jesus, I Boldly, I Fearlessly and I Confidently intercede on behalf of my friend. Lord, I pray that my friend will be filled with the Holy Spirit and healed from all illness. Father God, I am calling upon you asking you to completely heal and deliver my friend! I pray that my friend will give you all honor, praises and glorify your mighty name.

In the name of Jesus, It is you, who will completely deliver my friend from the pit and corruption of illness. My friend will no longer be held captive to the enemy! Lord, we know that you have not given my friend a spirit of depression, anxiety, anger, and sadness. My friend will not be moved by conflict and negative adversity, but You Lord have given my friend a spirit of love, calmness, patience, peace, and a well balanced mind, and self control.

In the name of Jesus, please forgive my friend's sins and stand in the gap for my friend until my friend is totally healed and delivered from all illness disorders, which has held my friend captive.

I break all generational curses off my friend's life now!
It is our mighty God who will totally heal and deliver.
I speak boldly in the name of Jesus that my friend is
healed, delivered and free from all illnesses.

My friend shall no longer be of two minds, unstable,
unreliable and uncertain about anything. My friend
is free of all anxiety, depression, poor temper control,
sadness and anger...
Thank you Lord for totally healing my friend!

This is my prayer in Jesus' name.
Amen, Amen and Amen.

My Intriguing Experience

On 8/8/08 the wait was finally over. She met that special man in person she had met only via the computer and telephone.

As she entered the baggage claim area in the Airport she looked around for his face but was unable to spot him. He walked up behind her and said "Hello" and she smiled as her heart bounded in her chest with excitement. She gazed upon his brown handsome face with a smile painted bright. He was tall, caramel chocolate, well dressed in her favorite color. Confident and handsome he was. They embraced with a long hug and somehow at that moment she knew God was directing their meeting. Silently, she said "Thank you Lord for being in control of my life".

As the hours and days went on she learned that he was not only "fine" but he is kind, attentive, fun, sensitive, strong, gentle, and a true gentleman. He made her smile, he made her laugh, he made her happy, and he made her feel beautiful by his kind words, hugs, and kisses. And, oh those big strong arms wrapped around her made her feel so safe. Her mind was so clear and she thought of only him and nothing else at that moment mattered.

Those three intriguing days she spent with him seemed as if she knew him for eternity. They connected instantly and shared long conservations with lots of smiles and laughs. They complimented each other with lots of hugs and kisses. It was electrifying, hot and steamy! Only something she had read about in a love novel. She asked herself, could this be love at first sight? Is it such a thing?? She started wondering if this was only a dream and she would wake up soon, because she had never experienced anything like this before in her life time. Then, in an instant she remembered that she had prayed for years to please send her Godly Soul mate who would take her breath away.

She is so blessed to have had the opportunity to meet such a kind gentleman, one who took her breath away. But, reality sets in and she realized that she lives 4, 800 miles away from him. She continued to pray, "Lord please send him back my way". Then she realized that he came to her life for a "Reason" and his reason is done! He has taught her all he can; now it's time for him to fade away in the sun.

She praised God . . . "Thank you Lord for allowing our path to cross as I know it was only the works of you, because I could have never planned such a perfect meeting with such a fine man".

Thank you, for such an Intriguing Experience even if it was just for a "Reason" and not a "Life time"!

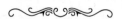

Celebrating Me

I am wonderfully made . . . I am beautiful, I am smart, I am attractive, I am fine, I am lovely, I am sexy, I am delightful, and I am cute!

I am an inspiration for others . . . I am a Godly woman, I am successful, I am a women of honor, I am special, I am a woman with favor, I am powerful and , I am blessed!

I am worthy for greatness . . . I am honest, I am peaceful, I am faithful, I am committed, I am loyal, I am dedicated, I am important, and I am strong!

Yes, I will celebrate me! And I don't need anyone to validate me. NO! Its not vanity or ego, its just reality because God made me!

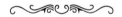

I am Uniquely Made

I appreciate who I am because I can only be me; I love me for being me! I love my brown radiant skin, I love my bright and pretty smile , I love my wide hips, I love my big butt, I love my thick thighs, I love my breast, I love my nappy hair, I love my big nose, I love my teeth, I love my loud voice, I love my dialect, I love my big lips, I love my big legs, I love my big brown eyes, I love my hands, I love my head, I love my crocket toes, I love my knocked knees, I love my love handles, I love my fat stomach, I love my size. I am wonderful just as I am; because I am one of a kind . . . I am uniquely made just for me!

Forgiveness Is Free

The hurt is so painful; it cuts deep in your soul. Your heart aches and aches, your eyes are red and swollen from crying; your voice hurts from yelling. You are devastated of the news! How could the person who loves you the most turns around and hurt you the worst? When you awake daily you are reminded of the hurt, pain and shame. When you try to hold up your head and face reality it seems so unbearable so you just continue to complain and complain. You are so ashamed and afraid to face the truth because reality is so hard to embrace sometimes; but you know you must face your fear and accept the truth about what hurt you! You have done nothing wrong and must not take on the burden of someone else wrong doing and evil ways.

Now, how do you practice true forgiveness and move on? Hold your head high and pray night and day. Walk in faith and speak of love and kindness in every way. Release your hurt, pride, and shame and forgive them in every way. For forgiveness is free and healing is only for your soul; freeing you to reach your goals. Yes, forgiveness is free let it go!

In The Meantime . . .

While we are separated, remember my Love that will last for eternity. Remember my Smile it's so bright and sweet. Remember my Prayers it brought healing to your soul. Remember my Support as I stood by your side. Remember my Words it was so true to you. Remember my Encouragements it uplifted you too. Remember my Laugh it was filled with joy. Remember my Gentle touches it was so soft just for you. Remember my Kisses, it was electrifying and sweet. Remember my Hugs, it reassured you. Remember my Scent it was as sweet as a gently breeze filled with strawberries. Remember my Walk with that little twist. Remember my Talk so sweet as can be to encourage you. Remember my Voice it calmed you daily. Remember my Face it was graced with beauty and truth. Remember my Truth as I told you I will always love you, but most of all please remember the God in me!

Why Are You Still Single?

She has learned that we date people for many different reasons . . . Physical attraction, friendship, companionship, social interactions, power, opportunities, excitement, fun, the need for acceptance, money, good looks, and love. She is well aware that many of her relationships will not be life time relationships but can be great learning experiences. Maybe that's why she is still single.

To be truly honest, sometimes she can be very guarded and find it hard to know if a man is really interested in "you" for "you" or if he is really the true person he is portraying himself to be. Other times she has noticed that some men are intimated by what he perceives as a successful, powerful, and unattainable sister. With that being said, many times it can be hard to find the right balance and that saddens her as a women. Maybe that's why she is still single.

Often times we date a man we think is Mr. Right and are God sent because he seems to have all the right answers and seems to match your life style. Only later we realized that he was sent only for a "Reason or a "Season" and not a "life time". It becomes very emotional and draining when yet another relationship ends. Maybe that's why she is still single.

As far as she is concerned, she just wants to be viewed as an ordinary woman who is "extraordinary" in many areas of her life and admired for her positive personal qualities, and inner beauty. She wants to be a good help mate, she would love to find a man who is truly committed to giving unconditional love and being 100 % committed. Not one who will break under pressure, give up when adversities come and walk out on her when things get tough. Maybe that's why she is still single.

She would be lying if she refused to admit that a "good and comfortable life style" with the finer things added is not what she aspire and believe she deserves. But, she is well aware that all of the successes and riches in her life mean nothing if she doesn't have someone special to share it with, or if she never finds her soul mate to truly share true unconditional love. Maybe that's why she is still single.

So today she journey along in her life, mostly alone remaining positive and embracing every opportunity and experiences both good and bad as a learning lesson. She is patiently waiting with faith, hope and assurance that her devoted Godly soul mate will find her one day soon, but until that time comes she will live her life to the fullest and continue to prepare herself for his arrival. That's why she is still single.

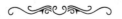

Think About It!

*Why do we give up so quickly? Is it because we don't
have FAITH! Where is your faith my child of God?
"Faith is the substance of things hoped for, the evidence
of things not seen". Did you know that "without faith
it is impossible to please God, for he who comes to God
must believe that He is and that He is a rewarded of
those who diligently seek Him"? Have more FAITH!*

*Is it because we don't PRAY like we should! We must
pray and have faith that God will answer our prayers.
Pray until something happens. Pray, watch, and wait.
PRAY more!*

*Is it because we don't have PATENCE! We don't know
how to tolerate trying circumstances in our life. We
must be able to tolerate being hurt, provoked, or
annoyed without complaint, losing our temper and
giving in so quickly. Have more PATENCE!*

*Is it because we don't know how to FIGHT for what we
want. We should stand up and fight. Never give up and
never give in!*

*Is it because we don't give UNCONDITIONAL
LOVE? We must love our friends and family with
unconditional love. We should have no conditions
or limitations on our love. It should be guaranteed,
with no conditions, limitations, or provision attached.
Practice true unconditional love!*

Think about it . . . The root cause of our issues is we don't give God a chance to work out our problems and fight our battles . . . We have no faith, we don't pray like we should, we have no patience to wait, we don't know how to stand up and fight for what we want, we give up and give in too soon and we don't give unconditional love to our friends and family. We should, think about it before we start!

Let It Go

Oh, how I loved my man! I love him today and I always will love him; but I had to let go! I stood up and made a drastic decision to break the cycle of the bad behaviors and habits in the relationship. I had to let it go!

This hurt so much to have to do this. I prayed to God for a sure sign on what to do. The next day he was gone again. I was so broken, empty, and deeply hurt I had to let go!

I started guarding my heart and that created problems with lack of affection for my man. I found myself not believing in him or trusting him with my heart completely. I lost all hope for saving our relationship when he walked out on me once again; I just could not take the rejections and deep pain anymore. I had to let it go!

I had to break the vicious cycle of negativity and disrespect. I lost me and he lost him, we both lost ourselves in the negativity. The drama became too much and we didn't know how to move forward in love. I had to let go!

I became a negative angry woman that I did not recognized nor did I like. I lost myself and felt helpless in the fight. "When one becomes helpless she is unable to help ones self or help anyone else". I had to let it go!

I felt like I was at war in my head. It was like being on a fast emotional roller coaster spinning out of control and I began to live in fear, I felt paralyzed and could not rise up to my full potential. I had to let go!

I never wanted fear to take over my life, but it did because I never knew when he was going to leave me again. I had to let go!

Getting the strength and courage to walk away was one of the hardest things I have ever had to do. I love him so much, but I love myself more! I had to let it go!

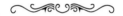

Power of Prayer

You must pray everyday just to find your way. Pray morning, noon and night then some more and don't let nothing or nobody stand in your way. Pray, watch and wait for I am sure God will answer things in his way. Don't let those people tell you "NO" God will work it out I know. I don't care what those people say nor do God will work it out for you!

If By Chance

*Will I see you again? I love you and miss you so much!
I miss your presence, kisses and gentle touch. You were
the love of my life. You brought so much excitement and
you taught me so much about true love. You inspired
me to grow and do more. You gave me my wings to fly
high. I wish we could start all over and go back to those
days when love came freely. But I do understand that
living in the past is not reality. Be sure to remember all
the fun things we shared and how we prayed together.
Remember all the great memories we made together
and special times we shared. Remember what God said,
"We belong together". If by chance we meet again, I
will be sure to say "I Love YOU"!*

She Ain't Me

Can't you see she can't compare to me. My classiness and style is apparent and seen so vividly. My Godliness stands bold as I pray for you and with you every day. I secretly intercede on your behalf while you sleep.

I lift you high and hold you tight just to keep you protected from the enemy. I am the dedicated one who will never cheat. Please don't be fooled by her pretentious ways, it will surly make you go astray. Believe me, with her it's only the 80/20 you will reap, because she "Ain't" me!

Thought For Today . . .

One thing for sure is, as you live you will go through mighty storms in your life, so it really doesn't matter what you are going through today if you are grounded in the Lord. But what really matters and what will truly define your character and your faith is the way you react and act when going through the storms of life. Don't let the mighty storms of life sweep you away . . . Stay grounded in the Lord.

Stay strong & encouraged today my brothers and sisters!

Stop the Negativity

Why do you hate your brothers and sisters and become so negative? We must stop hating on our brothers and sisters and help them when we can. Don't you know that our country will be a better place if we just let love in our hearts? We should learn how to celebrate our brothers and sisters success and not pull them down and create more stress.
So many people are jealous of someone else's success. Don't they know that they can be blessed themselves? We must stop the negativity before we all go down in this mess!

When you gossip about people's business and keep up mess, it hurts even the best. How could you lie on people's name just to get ahead in the game? You should be so ashamed. Tell me, how can you backstab your friends and smile in their face just to make you look good again? This mess has to end! Why do you hold grudges and let it eat you up for years? Don't you realize that makes you sick and full of fear? Can we just practice true forgiveness when someone makes a mistake? I'm sure that would be a start for a better place. We most stop this negativity so we all can be blessed!

What makes them so bitter and angry and keep a frown on their face night and day? Don't they know bitterness can take you astray? How can you harbor resentment day after day, and then allow pride and ego to get in the way. How can you hold prejudice in your heart so deep that allows you to judge others right from the start, even before you meet? We must stop this negativity before it destroys you and me!

Why are we so negative in this country criticizing our President and leaders publicly? Don't you know that brings controversy, hate and misery? We must stop the negativity before it destroys our country!

Why don't we pray for President Obama and help him to rise, so He can take our great country on high. Don't we all want to survive?
Your negativity is hurting you, me and this country. Let's do it all in the power of love . . . . Stop the Negativity!

Family Prayer

In the name of Jesus, I declare a miracle in my family's life right now! I speak healing, deliverance, and total peace from God our Father. Lord, your word said: anything we ask in the name of Jesus it shall be done. You said if we have faith of a mustard seed we could move a mountain. Lord I believe your words and I come to you today with mighty faith expecting a miracle for my family. Lord I praise you and thank you for your favor over my family's life. I love you Lord and I Love my family. I thank you for your unconditional love and your total forgiveness. In the mighty name of Jesus, by your stripes my family is healed and delivered from all generational curses and captivities! God we give you all honor and praises in the mighty name of Jesus. Amen, Amen and Amen!

Daddy's Strength

You are strong and you are mighty! And yes, you are so great and wonderful to me. I look up to you for guidance and leadership with great power, truth and honesty.

You are the epitome of strength and the definition of hope and honor. Your faith is so strong, it shows in all you do and say. You look like a miracle and you are successful in all you do. God's favor is on your life and yes He blessed you too. You inspire others to dream big and do the impossibilities.

You show unconditional love to all and lead by examples for everyone who is watching. You handle adversity and suffering well. You never gave up because you have a story to tell!

You are a courageous man who prays and prays for everyone even when you are down. Your caring spirit stands out; you care for all that is around. You always give an encouraging word to those who need it most. Even through sickness and suffering, you always gave of yourself and served others the most.

You have taught us to never give up and never give in regardless of what it looks like we have to win. You have hope for God promises when it seems all hope is gone.

Your faith in the Lord is so strong; you speak it in existence for all to see. You are a strong faithful servant of God deeply rooted in His words with unshakable faith! You are a mighty blessing for everyone you come in contact with.

You are truly worthy to be praised for your strength and lessons you share on your journey.

Tribute to Mommy

*Mommy, you are all I ever wanted to be! Your strength
and coverage is so unique to me. You always make
things better when we can't seem to find our way; some
how you always know what to say. You stand on the
truth and never give in. You guide us and mold us in a
Godly way; and yes, you pray for us night and day.*

*Your love is so unique and real that all of your children
can feel your warmth from deep within. You are sweeter
than honey and more valuable that anyone's money.*

*You are like diamonds and pearls more valuable than
anything in this entire world. You are like pure gold,
shinning so bright in the light giving us love everyday of
your life.*

*Mommy's love is authentic and unconditional in
everyway. She will climb the highest mountain and
swim the longest ocean for her children so don't get in
her way. She gives her children the world looking for
nothing in return.*

*Mommy's love is so gentle and kind and she is always
on time. She never lets us down and teaches us how to
be strong. She leads by example working so hard just to
make things happen for all. She gives of herself like no
one else can give.*

Mommy's love is so patient and understanding. She loves us more and more everyday even when we make her cry. For we know that Mommy's love comes from on high in the sky.

Thank you Mommy for being our everything and more. If we can just be half of what you are we would be so mighty to see. You are who we aspire to be even the more. Mommy, we Love you for eternity!

A Sister's Love

*Yes! She loves me so much and its authentic love. A
sister's love is one that is unique to see. Her love, care,
and concerns, are obvious for all to see. She is my
advocate and support team who never lets me down
even if I do wrong. She protects me from the mean
cruel world by giving me advice and warns me of the
unknown. Together we overcame many adversities and
obstacles which made us stronger. We share many family
secrets we dare to tell anyone else. We are sometimes
judged but we never give in to the world's definition
us. We are mighty sisters of faith who prays and prays
before we do anything. She is family and she sticks with
me through thick and thin until the end. Through many
challenging life experiences we cried together, we laughed
together, we learned together, and we prayed together.
She is my rock and truth and she keeps me in tune with
reality. She is my cheerleader, who cheers for my victory!
A sister's love is authentic and unique for all to see.*

A Loving Son

He is a meek and mild man with a big Heart. His bright smile lights up any room he graces. His calm and cool composure is his signature style. His happiness and kindness shines through in all he does as he gives of himself. His inner and outer beauty captures all attention from close and far. He works hard for what he wants and never gives up until he reaches his goals. My loving son puts God first in all he does so he knows he is a step above. He tries hard and prays more. He prays before he makes any big decisions right from the start. He is a man of strength and honor any woman would desire. He always shows love and respect for all he meets, which makes him stand tall. He shows great love for his mother everyday. He loves her with all of his heart and he always tells her she is the best "Mommy" in the world. He has a special bond with his father too, which will last for eternity. Thank God for a true blessing; a fine, smart, and handsome loving son!

Lady Preacher

You are a phenomenal woman, yes you are. Thank you for being such a positive role model for all of the ladies around you. You have allowed us to see what we can become. With elegance, truth and faith you touched our lives in such a positive and profound way. You inspired us to become more and to continue to reach for our goals and pray. You taught us to not allow negative situations to turn us away and to stand tall with grace and faith during adversities. You motivated us everyday to get up and go and get what we wanted. You lead by example so we all can see what a true lady preacher should be. You are down to earth and believable in all you do and say. You are not perfect but great in many ways. The love you share for all is wonderful and contagious to see. You are a great inspiration and a breath of fresh air for everyone you meet. We enjoyed your powerful preaching and teaching and took heed. You are a fire cracker that keeps us on the edge of our seat every time you teach and preach. You keep it real so we all can see and feel what a phenomenal woman can be.

I Trust You . . .

I trust that you will take care of me!
I trust that you will support me!
I trust that you would never hurt me!
I trust that you will never cheat on me!
I trust that I am the only one you want!
I trust that you will be honest with me!
I trust that you are waiting on me!
I trust that you can't wait to see me!
I trust that you will add to my happiness!
I trust that you love me!
I trust that you will pray for me!
I trust that you will never leave me!
I trust that you will be mine and only mine one day!
I trust you Today, Tomorrow and A Lifetime!

Wings of True Love

The essence of something so great and so sweet is truly what completes me. My love is strong and happy with tender affection I feel deep within me. The pure and honest substance surrounds me with intensity. It grows and grows and blossoms into a great big beautiful romantic rose. If it's bottled up it will erupt into an explosion of colors of creativity. Oh, how my passion grows every minute, every hour, every day; its deep emotions imbedded so far in my heart that I feel when we are near and apart. The attraction is so strong it keeps my heart burning with desires for you and only you. Your enthusiasm lifts me to a higher place. It takes me on a journey to the stars and moon and brings me back to see your enchanting face. Your romantic ways keeps my heart beating and beating with expectations of greatness and curiosity of what comes next. It sweeps me off my feet and takes me to a fantasy Island where only you and I exist. My imagination shows our romantic affair which keeps me floating on air. It's something eliciting that brings me to a world of completeness and happiness.

A Special Meeting on 12/13/09

On 12/13/09 I met a special man that changed my life
forever! Our eyes met with mystery and I smiled as my
heart leaped in my chest with excitement. He stood with
confidence as we embraced with a hug. We steered into
each other's eyes with curiosity and drafted away into
the moon light. Somehow at that moment I knew that
God was coming through with something special for me.

As days, months and a year passed; I learned that he
was not only a fine southern man but he was one of
a kind, rare and true. He was very romantic giving
me flowers everyday, very caring and attentive to my
every need. He prayed with me, and for me. He went to
church with me too. He made me very happy; he made
me feel special in every way. He told me I was beautiful
and smart every day! He even told me that he loved me
and wanted no one else, so I should stay.

The special time I spent with him seemed as if I knew
him for a life time. He treated me like royalty; giving
me all I wanted and needed. We grew closer and closer
in a positive way so I knew God sent him my way.

He taught me so much about love and life, pushing me
to greater height. He inspired me to reach my goals, and
taught me how to fly high you know. We shared long
talks about our goals and dreams. He encouraged me
and inspired me everyday. He helped me and supported
me in so many different ways. He was everything
I always wanted in a man and I knew it was only
something God could bring together in His plan.

As I floated on air, I wondered, could this be the man for me and will it last for eternity? Then I was reminded that I prayed for years to please send me my Godly man who would adore me and love me more for all time.

Suddenly with no one to blame, despite the greatness the passion could not sustain; it faded away . . . oh what a shame! In my curiosity, I prayed night and day asking will my man go or stay. Just as I am about to lose all hope, I heard my angel speak softly saying "Never give up hope! If this is truly God's plan, nothing or no one can keep us apart, for there is nothing that God's plan can't withstand"

Thank you God for blessing me to have had this opportunity to meet such a special man. He is one whom I think of often and longing to grace his presence again. If by chance we should meet again I am sure he will make me complete.

I praise God for sending him my way, even though he was only here in my life for a "Season" and not a "Life Time" Despite it all, I know for sure it was only the works of our "Angels" allowing our path to cross, because I could have never planned such a perfect meeting with such a special and caring man! Our meeting has served its purpose and he had to go, but he still makes my passion flow! I wonder does he know.

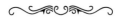

He Was Made For Me Exclusively

You think I can't see she wants my man? I'm sure it's because he treats me as a queen, a queen just as I am. Girl you can't replace me, you don't have what it takes to compare to me. My man was made for me, only me exclusively!

God ordained our love, directed our path, and orchestrated our meeting so he was made especially for me, only me exclusively

You don't have my style and favor from God; you must realize that I prayed to God for years to send him my way, we are a perfect match by God that's sacred to thee. You should pray for your own man and He will bless you in the same way as me. He was made for me, only me exclusively!

Girl, don't waste your time trying to change his mind and trying to replace me. My man and I have something special; it's uniquely; a bond so tight it's sealed with God's approval and love for eternity. He was made for me, only me exclusively!

I have nothing to lose and you have nothing to gain so please stop playing those evil games! Don't you see God is not pleased with you? He said, "Let no man separate what I have joined together" Now stop making yourself look ashamed, don't mess with God's plan and leave my husband alone! He was made for me for eternity, only me exclusively!

I Apologize!

I am so sorry! Please let me take this opportunity to apologize to you again; with sincere heart. I am truly sorry for all hurt, pain and disappointments I have caused you. Please forgive me forever! Forgive my pettiness for I am an imperfect woman.

I pray to God for forgiveness daily and to search my heart and remove anything that is not pleasing to Him. In my prayer I asked God to replace it with unconditional love, kindness, gentleness, and patience to live deep within me. Dear Lord, please make me a better person for eternity!

If Dr Martin Luther King can forgive injustice surly you can forgive me, for I am only human with imperfections. I apologize . . . Please forgive me!

Thank You!

I am forever grateful for you! Your act of caring and kindness will never be forgotten. I am overjoyed that you went over and beyond just for me. Words cannot express my appreciation of your kindness and thoughtfulness. Thank you for your concerns and prayers when I needed it most. You interceded on my behalf and held me high with prayers. You stood by my side when I cried and told me to continue to try.

I give you my heartfelt appreciation for the beautiful words of encouragement and motivation you bestowed upon me. It uplifted my spirit and stirred my passion to become more like you. You have inspired me to reach deep inside and give more of myself. Your attentiveness has motivated me to reach higher and unleash my creativity even the more. Your kindness and caring spirit will forever be ingrained in my heart and mind. Your act of confidence inspired mankind. Again, I extend my gratitude to you for giving of yourself without being selfish and expecting nothing in return. You are a true example of what compassion should be.

I Survived

I am a survivor! I wash all my tears and disappointments away today. I throw away shame and pity. See, it's a new day, and no one can get in my way. I survived it all; heart break, pain, hurt, and lies. The storm is finally over. Yes! I survived!

So many tried to break me, but they can't stop me. I emerged with power and strength and indulged myself with the promises I knew from the start. I can't look back and I wouldn't let go for the Lord told me so.

You thought that I would break down and die; you wanted me to fail. But look at me now with all my blessings and favor as I rocket to the sky flowing on top of the world. It's obvious that I still have it all as I still stand tall.

As the sun shines bright, so do I. Today is a new day filled with excitement, joy and anticipation. A new beginning with many new opportunities is in my reach, for today is a better day. I survived it all and Yes! I still stand tall!

Edwards Brothers, Inc.
Thorofare, NJ USA
September 12, 2011